Nora Naranjo-Morse

MUD WOMAN

Poems from the Clay

The University of Arizona Press

Tucson

Third printing 1997
The University of Arizona Press
Copyright © 1992
Nora Naranjo-Morse
All Rights Reserved
Printed in Hong Kong

00   99   98   97   6   5   4   3

Library of Congress Cataloging-in-Publication Data

Naranjo-Morse, Nora, 1953–
   Mud woman : poems from the clay / Nora Naranjo-Morse.
     p.   cm. — (Sun tracks ; v. 20)
   ISBN 0-8165-1248-5 (cl.). — ISBN 0-8165-1281-7 (pbk.)
   1. Pueblo Indians—Poetry.   2. Pueblo Indians—Pottery—Poetry.
I. Title.   II. Series.
PS3564.A67M8   1992   91-16611
811′.54—dc20   CIP

British Library Cataloguing-in-Publication Data
A catalogue record for this book is available from the British Library.

Frontispiece: *Heeng chae Kosa, micaceous clay, 1990.*

MUD WOMAN

Volume 20

SUN TRACKS

An American Indian Literary Series

Series Editors

Larry Evers and Ofelia Zepeda

Editorial Committee

Vine Deloria, Jr.

Joy Harjo

N. Scott Momaday

Emory Sekaquaptewa

Leslie Marmon Silko

For Greg

Contents

Preface

For hundreds of years Pueblo people have treasured their powerful relationship with clay. Veins of colored earth run along the hillsides of New Mexico, covering remote trails with golden flecks of mica. Channels of brown and scarlet mud wash across the valleys, dipping and climbing with the sprawling landscape. Intricately woven patterns of clay fan out under the topsoil, carrying the life of pottery to the Pueblo people.

Initially, the Towa (people) gathered this mud and processed it to make vessels for day-to-day use. Family members ventured out to surrounding foothills that held this precious commodity. Even today, when a vein is located and uncovered, a prayer is offered to Nan chu Kweejo (Clay Mother), acknowledging her generous gifts to us:

Nan chu Kweejo,
na ho uvi whageh oe powa,
di huu joni heda di aweh joni
hey bo hanbo di koe gi un muu.
Wayhaa ka yun un maa bo,
wi un tsi maai pi.

Clay Mother,
I have come to the center of your
   abode,
feed me and clothe me
and in the end you will absorb me
into your center.
However far you travel,
do not go crying.

This prayer continually renews our relationship to the earth, her gifts, and Towa.

Nan chu Kweejo invites me to celebrate in a unique and limitless form of cultural expression. Sounds of clay slowly filtering through sifting screens, mud slapping rhythmically against open palms, even the wild popping of cedar when firing pottery all become important elements of celebration. Subtle lessons from Clay Mother awaken my appreciation for daily rituals, connecting me to the Pueblo worldview. A Ladybug explores the caverns of a clay form on my worktable. I offer her direction across the moist, cool surface. In doing so, I hear my echo, deep in the walls of coiled earth. I am no more or less than the Ladybug. Her presence is a gift to my studio. Hearing my echo, I am reminded of an essential element in the Pueblo worldview.

Plant, animal and human life cycles, nurtured and guarded, are held equally in a larger vessel called earth. The symmetry of earth's vessel depends on our respect for earth's balance and our caretaking of these cycles. Gathering this knowledge as I do clay, I am impressed by the spiritual strength of these lessons. This cultural rooting encourages me when I explore my own creative vein. I am excited and challenged by simple lines, new shapes, and textures. I weave my experiences as a modern Pueblo woman into this fiber of clay work, centuries old.

Every day, clay is a part of my routine. I move easily in and out of any one of the many steps included in completing an earthen form. Soaking mud, sieving it through screens, draining excess water, mixing in volcanic ash with bare feet—each step is time-consuming and laborious. People unaware are surprised by all that is involved in clay work. Every finished piece holds a history of culture and time, and of constant, caring attention. The hours invested preparing the gathered mud are important for readying pliable clay and for preparing myself for the creative process. The simple act of doing opens creative channels. Time is measured only by the sifted buckets of volcanic ash. I sieve long enough in one place that ants march freely across my feet.

Unharried work opens my mind to imagination. I travel with the ants as they busy themselves collecting building supplies; their body forms and movements become my creative inspiration. Unspoken ties connecting me to clay strengthen and clear a path for thoughtful awareness of my surrounding. Birds call to one another from across an open field. I stop to listen to their hellos, and I am impressed by the multitudes of life cycles thriving continuously on just an ordinary day.

Gia (mother) has been an influential part of my commitment to clay. I remember her nimble fingers curving in and around smooth surfaced bowls. As a child I was her helper, learning the skill and method of pottery from her example. There were never measurements or formal instruction, rather stories introducing Nan chu Kweejo's powerful presence, and motherly advice about my sagging jars or crooked bowls. Gia's manner of instruction, cultural teachings, and spirited determination planted the seed of dreaming an idea and cultivating it to fruition. Baking bread, raising children, sculpting in mud, dreams large or small are valuable as daily rituals for a life flowing with creativity.

In preparation, I knead handfuls of clay as images of people, their gestures, city skylines, the ocean, television noise, and more fill my thoughts. Uncensored imagination, along with the purity of childlike play, explodes on my worktable.

Layered coils begin to build and drain my supply of all that I absorb as a human being, a Pueblo woman, a mother, wife, and friend. The micaceous and Santa Clara clays I use are porous and absorb water quickly into their mass. At times I feel the essence of who I am being digested in each coil, connecting me forever to each piece and again reminding me of the symmetry of life cycles that Towa hold sacred.

From journeys across oceans, experiencing other world-views, to enlightening trips to the grocery store, people and their ways fuel my curiosity, inspire, and continuously educate me. Traveling has given me the opportunity to appreciate my tradition even more. I carry my cultural rooting proudly, sharing it, and in return, receiving unforgettable moments that feed my awareness as a human being.

While teaching in Germany, I traveled by train with my four-year-old daughter and two hundred pounds of clay. I was unable to understand the language, and the train system completely perplexed me. I was lost and afraid of missing my next train. Taking pity on me, two older travelers, both sturdy, matriarchal-looking women, approached us. They spoke German. Relieved by any type of assistance, I handed them our tickets and shrugged. Surmising our situation in an excited exchange, both women gathered my daughter and the bags of clay and pulled me hurriedly to the train.

Pushing us into closing doors, neither woman stopped talking as they waved good-bye. Tears welled in my eyes as I tried to thank them; they knew, without words, my appreciation. I wanted to tell these German women that they reminded me of my aunts in another village far away. Moments like this, as well as other experiences, are intrinsic to my creative process. With so much of myself invested, oftentimes it has been difficult to let go of my work. I liken it to older mothers letting go of their children who are anxious to leave the nest for their own life's flight.

In recent years, the popularity of Pueblo pottery has escalated to such a degree that the effects of demand have shifted, changing the more natural course of our clay methods. Our relationship to Nan chu Kweejo and the symmetry of the Pueblo worldview, conflict many times with the dominant society's values, values that encourage the demand and commercialism of Pueblo pottery. Seventy years ago, when Gia was a child, Towa worked together, making large storage bowls for communal food supplies. Energy and skill were shared in molding magnificent vessels for the common good of all villagers. Today the act of creating has become an individualized process, limiting, for the most part, an important element of community exchange.

While growing up in the fifties and early sixties, curio shops were a familiar sight. They dotted reservation borders along highways well traveled by motoring tourists. These establishments became increasingly popular, serving as a profitable outlet for Gia and other Pueblo women selling their pottery. Loudly colored Thunderbirds and other stereotypical Indian designs, decorated curio store fronts. Tourists were welcome to come and see "live Indians" demonstrate their crafts right in the store. It was not unusual to see Navajo men stamping silver jewelry on a worktable conveniently set up by the coke machines. Fluorescent tomahawks and plastic war bonnets were sold alongside rubber spiders and slides of the Southwest. Postcards of the proud Navajo herding sheep into an orange sunset sold for a dime, next to the images of historical buildings in Santa Fe.

On the days we ventured into the curio stores to sell Gia's pottery, storeowners attempted polite conversation while scrutinizing her black, polished vases. Tapping each bowl for a ring would determine how well they were fired and whether or not there were surface cracks. With furrowed brow, the owner pointed out flaws, which to him devalued the pot. If a particular shape or pattern of design became popular and sold quickly, Gia was asked to bring several more of the same on her next visit. The look of confusion on Gia's face when trying to comprehend an arbitrary standard for work she had done most of her life is forever printed in my mind. The poem, "Mud Woman's First Encounter with the World of Money and Business," characterizes similiar, present-day attitudes toward a finished clay form.

Several summers ago, during a weekend arts and crafts show, I was impressed at how greatly business influences Native American art. Thousands of dollars changed hands during two days of selling. Pottery, painting, and jewelry were only a few of the art categories judged. Ribbons were handed out for artwork considered the best in its division. Top prizes validated artists to collectors who bought award-winning pieces at astronomical prices. Some parents sold their children's artwork for unreasonable sums, suggesting to buyers that first pieces from a budding artist might be a worthwhile investment. A frenzy of buying blanketed the booths of art as hundreds of people clamored to see the Indians and their artwork. In all of this I wondered how my people's creative integrity would survive.

My work does not generally conform to standards set by the present Indian art market. I exercise my creative licence in a menagerie of characters that travel through time, inspired by culture and personal experiences. The results are forms like Pearlene, whose thirst for adventures educate her to life's lessons. Pearlene fluctuates between confusion and clarity, reverence and mischief, while searching for her niche in life.

The frequency of her presence on my worktable symbolized personal life situations and the resulting explosion of new ideas. Pearlene tested new waters in my creative growth, challenging stereotypical perceptions dictated by the market for Pueblo pottery.

After a slide and poem presentation on Pearlene's importance in my creative growth, a retired schoolteacher from the Midwest approached me. Winking, nudging me gently, she whispered, "Honey, I'm a Pearlene, too." That whispered confession enlightened me to the universal appeal of art. Pearlene was the connecting link between that teacher and me for a few memorable moments. These precious moments serve as nutrients in my life, inspiring my creative approach. Pearlene became popular. At poetry readings, people were anxious to hear of her latest adventures. Gallery owners requested Pearlene in salable sizes for the Christmas rush.

A businessman from California offered to mass produce Pearlene; however, the image of my clay friend in plastic, lining curio shops across the Southwest, frightened me. The effects of demand once again threatened to alter the flow of my natural creative process. Realizing her charm might be jeopardized by demand, I coiled one last Pearlene. My decision to explore new avenues of creative expression marked a milestone, which was symbolized in this last piece. In making her, I also coiled a companion for Pearlene. The balance created by adding another person in the final Pearlene would now permit me to close this chapter with a sense of dignity for both of us. In doing this, I began to understand the phenomena that has taken place for generations between Earth and Towa. The influence of this relationship continually fuels my desire to create, and in that desire I have found life-giving nourishment. I am a vessel coiled by layers of life's experiences.

In the Tewa language, there is no word for art. There is, however, the concept for an artful life, filled with inspiration and fueled by labor and thoughtful approach.

The process of recording my life through clay and poetry results in an exciting volley of creative expression for me. Three-dimensional clay Pearlenes were often inspired by poems written months or even years before. In return, poems began to formulate images, complete with personality, physical detail, and motive. This collection of poems and clay forms documents a fifteen-year milestone of creating, fueled by life's gifts. From Nan chu Kweejo to the matriarchs in the German train station, all continually add to my possibilities for an artful life.

I gratefully acknowledge all my brothers and sisters, who, in their own way, supplied me with endless memories and a powerful foundation for these words: especially my sisters, Rina Swentzell and Dolly Naranjo and my brothers Tito and Michael Naranjo for their support and objective criticism. Special thanks goes to Vickie Downey, Laura Tohe, and Larry Evers, as well as to Zakary and Eliza, who feed me daily with life-giving nourishment, koo da wah haa.

MUD WOMAN

WHEN MUD WOMAN BEGINS

Electricity
    down my arm
    through this clay
    forming into
    spirit shapes
      of men
        women
        and children
        I have seen
        somewhere before.

Electricity
    surging upward
    as I mix
    this mud
    like my mother
      as her mother did
      with small
      brown feet.

Folding into this earth
    a decision of
    joyful play,
    transcending expectations
    of fear
      failure
      or perfection.

Creating spirits
    calling invitations
    of celebration.
    What occurs
    in completed form,

bright
  and bold,
  is motion
  from our mother's skin.

I smile
  momentarily satisfied
  with my play.
  Electricity,
  generated from star colors
  far from home,
  entering
    through my feet
    blessing my hands
    and opening my heart.

21

Mud Fetish

22   *Pinto Bean*
        and Grasshopper
        Ate My Lilacs
        and Didn't Even Care

CHILDLIKE ENTHUSIASM

It is not sophisticated technique or exact skill
    but childlike enthusiasm,
    timeless concentration
    and pure devotion that feed this clay to life for me.

Knowing this as my hands work slower than my desire to create,
feeling this on frigid winter mornings when clay spirits are
    cold and so am I.
Laughing in J.C. Penney's when I notice there is still clay
    stubbornly stuck under my fingernails,
        as I pass a free manicure display.

Dreaming up new shapes and stories for brown
    earth and me, as I secretly call myself
    Mud Woman.

Indulging in limitless, creative possibilities.
How lucky I am to know this clay.

WHEN THE CLAY CALLS

This clay starts calling to me only days after I've sworn it off
    wishing to leave tired hands to rest,
    wanting to release myself from the browns and reds
    that bend easily into gentle curves,
        instantly becoming a child's face,
        a woman's skirt, or her husband's smile.

Resting from lines I review,
    have reviewed,
        and will review again.

Dusting off the sanded earth
    as coarse surfaces level into fluid forms
    I had not yet discovered,
    so smooth and yet richly textured with life of its own.

I am in awe of this clay that fills me with passion
    and wonder.
    This earth
        I have become a part of,
        that also I have grown out of.

25

Landscape

Flat Fetishes

THERE IS NOTHING LIKE AN IDEA

There is nothing
  like an idea
    that comes to life
      through clay.
Each step
  a personal investment of
    thought
      labor
        and time.
Hands
  moving quickly,
    rounding curves
      setting up in clay
  skillful responses
    educated
      by Gia's
        simple instruction
          and immense knowledge
          of her own work.
Letting dreams come true
  from songs
    born from within,
      sounds
        inviting irresistible challenges.
There is nothing like an idea
  that comes to life
    through clay.
There is nothing better than a life
  whose dreams
    and ideas are
      just too
        impossible
          to resist.

THE LIVING EXHIBIT
UNDER THE MUSEUM'S PORTAL

Arriving with high hopes on a breezy March day
  to sell these forms I've made from clay.
  My pocketbook empty, as I lay my blanket down.
We arrive from all directions:
     Cochiti,
       Zuni,
         The Navajo
           and Pueblos.
Selling our blankets,
     bread
       and beads.
We bargain back and forth with tourists,
     and among ourselves . . .
     we must love to bargain.
My friend from Zuni tells me business is slow,
     as she keeps her hands busy, rearranging
     necklaces in single file, on black polyester.
     "Damn," she says, "to think, I could be sitting
     in a warm office right this minute, drinking
     hot chocolate and typing business letters
     for some honky."
A tourist and potential customer blurts out:
     "Excuse me, but do any of you Indians speak English?"
     I answer too politely, hating myself for doing so,
     thinking it must be my empty pocketbook
     talking for me.
The Indian tribes represented, line quietly against the stark,
     white museum wall, as each new day introduces
     throngs of tourists, filing past our blankets
     fixed in orderly fashion upon red bricks.
     Visitors looking for mementos to take home,

Kosa (Pueblo Clowns)
Poking Fun

that will remind them of the curiously
silent Indians, wrapped tightly in colorful
shawls, just like in the postcards.
Huddling together for warmth, we laugh, remembering
that sexy redhead last summer, who
bent down to pick up a necklace and
ripped her tight white pants.
Casually interested, we watch as Delbert, a city Indian,
hiding behind mirrored sunglasses,
pulls up at noon, to lay his blanket down.
He's come to sell brass and silver
earcuffs he and his girlfriend made.
Delbert sets up, while in the truck
his girlfriend sleeps off last night's party.
My friend is right, business is slow as the late afternoon breeze
hurries customers away from our blankets,
toward the Indian art galleries,
leaving us to feel the sting of cold
through layers of our woolen protection.
The sun fades into the Southwestern corner of the plaza
casting large, cold shadows that signal
the end of our day together.
Quietly we pack for home, bundling our wares
carefully in baskets and old grocery crates.
Back to:
    Cochiti,
        Zuni,
            The Navajo
                and Pueblos.
Tomorrow we will arrive, again with high hopes,
empty pocketbooks
        and our friendships right in place.

TRADITION AND CHANGE

My mission was to sell pottery from booth 109,
    so early that morning I drove to San Ildefonso.
I expected this market of arts and crafts to be full,
    a full day in many ways.
    Hundreds of steel-framed booths
    filled the center of the pueblo.
    Cars streamed in at a steady pace,
    while Summer's heat became relentless.
    Oh yes, and there were people, all kinds, from everywhere,
    looking to buy, with spend in their eyes.
    Maybe for pottery.
      I hoped so.
"Too expensive, Myrtle," I heard a man say to his wife,
    as she reached for one of my clay forms,
    his words pressing her onward to the next booth.
    If it was jewelry they were looking for, this was the place.
    Everything, from finely crafted turquoise inlaid bracelets
    to Mickey Mouse earrings set in mother of pearl,
    his nose in jet, and those shorts of Mickey's
    painted in coral stone.
The Summer's temperature rose as a loudspeaker
    blared continuous news of a disco dance
    being held that evening in another pueblo.
    Warning visitors to stay off the kiva steps,
    and reminding us that Navajo tacos were being sold
    at any one of eight refreshment stands
    along the outer wall of the village.
    A candidate for governor hurried by,
    shaking hands almost desperately
    with anyone who looked of voting age.
It was at that moment I turned away, trying to shake off
    this state I had entered.

32   *Water Jar on*
Mud Woman's
Head

You know, that state of mind that displaces you
for just a second.
Oh yes,
oh yes, this is San Ildefonso Pueblo in the 90's.
All this made me wonder where our people were headed,
what our ancestors would think about a Navajo Taco
going for $3.75.
I thought about changes affecting our tradition,
change and tradition,
on this hot, full day.

34   *Mud Woman's*
      First Encounter
      with the World of Money
      and Business

MUD WOMAN'S FIRST ENCOUNTER
WITH THE WORLD OF MONEY AND BUSINESS

She unwrapped her clay figures,
        unfolding the cloth each was nestled in,
        carefully, almost with ceremony.
        Concerning herself with the specific curves, bends and
        idiosyncrasies, that made each piece her own.
Standing these forms upright, displaying them from
        one side to the next, Mud Woman
        could feel her pride surging upward
        from a secret part within her,
        translating into a smile that passed her lips.
        All of this in front of the gallery owner.
After all the creations were unveiled, Mud Woman held her
    breath.
        The gallery owner, peering
        from behind fashionably designed
        bifocals, examined each piece
        with an awareness Mud Woman
        knew very little of.
        The owner cleared her throat, asking:
        "First of all dear, do you have a résumé? You know,
        something written that would identify you to the public.
        Who is your family?
        Are any of them well known in the Indian art world?"
Mud Woman hesitated, trying desperately to connect
        this business woman's voice with her questions,
        like a foreigner trying to comprehend
        the innuendos of a new language, unexpected
        and somewhat intimidating.
The center of what Mud Woman knew to be real
        was shifting with each moment in the gallery.

The format of this exchange was a new dimension
from what was taken for granted at home,
where the clay, moist and smooth,
waited to be rounded and coiled
into sensuous shapes, in a workroom
Mud Woman and her man had built
of earth too.
All this struggled against a blaring radio
with poor reception and noon hour
traffic bustling beyond the frame walls.
Handling each piece, the merchant quickly judged
whether or not Mud Woman's work would be a profitable
venture.
"Well," she began, "your work is
strangely different, certainly not traditional
Santa Clara pottery and I'm not
sure there is a market for
your particular style, especially
since no one knows who you are.
However, if for some reason you make it big,
I can be the first to say, 'I discovered you.'
So, I'll buy a few pieces and we'll see how it goes."
Without looking up, she opened a large, black checkbook,
quickly scribbling the needed information to make
the gallery's check valuable.
Hesitantly, Mud Woman exchanged her work for the
unexpectedly smaller sum that wholesale prices dictated.
After a few polite, but obviously strained pleasantries
Mud Woman left, leaving behind her
shaped pieces of earth.
Walking against the honks of a harried
lunch crowd, Nan chu Kweejo spoke:

"Navi ayu, ti gin nau na muu,
nai sa aweh kucha?"
"My daughter, is this the way it goes,
this pottery business?"
Hearing this, Mud Woman lowered her head,
walking against the crowd of workers
returning from lunch.
Nan chu Kweejo's question,
clouded Mud Woman's vision with a mist
of lost innocence,
    as she left the city
      and the world of
        money and business behind.

WANDERING PUEBLO WOMAN

WANDERING PUEBLO WOMAN

Wandering city streets,
    making tracks with the same feet on concrete,
    not Pueblo earth, but cold, hard cement.
    With the rest of the city wanderers,
    setting a pace.
      Fast,
        fast,
          past Radio City Music Hall,
          the World Trade Center and
          the studios where soap operas
          are taped.
Past begging bums
    and richly furred, spike-heeled, fashion plates.
    Mesmerized by an alluring city beat,
    combined seductively with the glamour
    of civilized humans, on every street corner.
    Giving in to the sensation of amazement
    that tilts your head back in disbelief,
    mouth open wide.
    Eyes searching for the sky,
    the sun that should have been there,
    beyond cement towers,
    canyons of glass covered walls,
      each with stories,
        hundreds and hundreds of stories.
My friend scolded me,
    "Keep your purse inside your coat, don't
    look in anyone's eyes, they'll think
    you're confronting them.
    Whatever you do, just keep moving."

This Pueblo woman turned city wanderer,
    storing each second of every sensation for stories,
      poems,
        pictures and forms,
          later on, when the city's pavement ends.
My head will reel and fall back,
again, mouth agape,
    with the same amazement,
      the same amazement,
        at the sky I can see now, even at night.
Coyotes greet me with cries, from the fields by Black Mesa.
    A million stars sparkle,
      as they welcome home their wandering Pueblo Woman.

43

Colors from the Heart

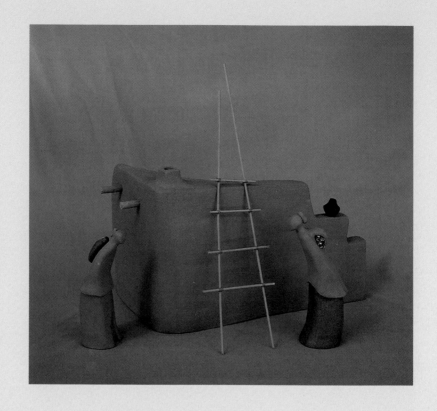

44

Towa

TOWA

Before communities of strangers settled,
    marking Pueblo boundaries
    and changing the arid
    open landscape forever,
    there were the people of Black Mesa,
        who called themselves Towa.
People whose clear, brown eyes witnessed
    star explosions high above them,
    against a celestial canvas of darkness.
    The Towa were filled with mystery,
        wonder
            and reverence
                for the universe encircling them.
    Reverence gave birth to ritual,
    celebration wove ceremony
    into songs that blanketed the village
    with life-giving spirit.
Planting nourishment for the children of Puye,
    with steady handwork,
    bedding seeds of corn,
        squash
            and beans.
Drum beats pounded upward,
    introducing a new season's fertile ground.
    Nimble fingers pressing seedlings into earth beds,
    Digging,
        planting,
            covering and smoothing
                in perpetual motion,
                    connecting each Towa
                        to the cycle of plant life.

45

From the heavens, to the rain-drenched earth beds,
    to the seedlings ripened into colored corn.
From the harvest to the Corn Dance.
      Clay-skinned people,
      danced with willowlike movements,
      then melted quietly into waiting earth beds.
      Seedlings creating another
        and yet another of these Towa.
      The plant and human life cycle,
        equal in symmetry.
This was before change disrupted night's mystery
      and other world views crowded into Pueblo boundaries.
      Now Towa rush to their jobs outside of village walls,
      adapting to standards unlike their own.
      Dressing our clay-skinned bodies
      in image conscious fashion,
      we stroke this new life of comfort.
Yet, somewhere in us,
      persistent sounds surge upward
      reminding us of our life cycles,
        and the innocent wonder
          that is our birthright,
            as children of the Towa.

TWO WORLDS

Yes, I'll admit it,
    I was by the water,
      on the beach,
        in the hot Pacific sun.
Turquoise water plunging to shore,
    as Palm trees undulate in time.
    Cold coconut drink in hand,
    I was sure I had stepped
    into a postcard from the tropics.
Suddenly,
    a dark cloud moved over me,
    appearing in this blue,
    guiltless sky.
    I started thinking:
    "Damn, Indian women,
    especially Pueblo women,
    don't drink Pina Coladas
      on Kauai beaches
        in December and enjoy it!"
    Scrutinizing other vacationers,
I wondered if they too felt dark
      clouds.
    Speaking in a language from across the water,
    "Meda cuna chaa,
    Meda cuna chaa."
    Was it true, had I forgotten who I was,
    where I'd come from?
    "Heda to an unde ung muu?
    Te ung unde we meda cuna ung muu."
    "And who do you think you are, a white person?"
    My sister's voice coming from the cloud above.
    Richly designed condos

dotted the sandy beaches,
dissimilar to unaffected mud structures
growing out of parched Pueblo land.
Even the scattered sunbathers,
in various shades of tan
seemed different than I.
Here I was,
   an Indian woman,
      enjoying herself in another world,
         among a different breed of people.
These thoughts collected,
causing me to feel anxious and uncertain.
When I was young,
we thought only Meda cuna took
luxurious vacations to exotic places . . .
Indians didn't.
Towa were supposed to stay home,
carrying on a tradition,
   separate from the rest of the world,
     this was our way.
Unlike the characteristically
homebound Towa,
I now had grown comfortable
in venturing out of Pueblo boundaries.
I wondered if there was a balance for me.
Where was my place in these opposing worlds?
Would I find it here,
   under the hot Pacific sun,
     or at home

48
        in the canyon's peaceful shelter?
The look on my face,
clued my husband,

**Black and White
Fetish**

49

he knows me very well.
With comforting words,
    he reminded me to enjoy
    every second of our day . . .
    to forget what was crossing me.
I eased into thought,
    consoling myself,
    reassessing my place in these worlds.
     I am a brown woman,
      who will always be a Towa,
       even under a hot Pacific sun.

THE MONEY BEASTS

I marvel at cashiers,
    how they handle those money beasts called
      cash registers.
Fingernails dipped in red polish,
punching incredible sums
with familiarity and skill,
picking from the beast's belly,
    amounts dictated for return.
Fantasizing what it would be like,
    if I too were entrusted with a company uniform.
      Suited in a two-piece polyester
        of brown and gray,
          allowing me into the inner world
            of fifties and hundreds.
Patiently waiting as customers
    forget cash
      or drop change.
Handling the uncomfortable message
    with directness . . .
"Sorry ma'am, we can no longer accept your checks."
This to the embarrassed housewife,
children in tow,
whose only recourse is to leave the store,
    empty-handed,
      branded.
The housewife exampling to other customers,
correct protocol in feeding the money beast,
    lest they suffer the same humiliation.
Loyal employees would quickly label me,
    "suspicious."
      Questioning my true allegiance,

52

*She Doesn't Come
from Around Here*

        as I side with customers
        whose purchases exceed their coupons.
Occasionally allowing kids with candy
        to slip through the counting grate,
        supplying my own change for their sweets.
Sooner or later I would get caught,
        stripped of my uniform
        humiliated,
            forced to join ranks with the housewife.
My only allowed participation,
        to feed the money beast.
I marvel at cashiers.

SOMETIMES I AM A SPONGE

Sometimes I am a sponge,
    pores open wide to receive liquid called life,
    in its essence an almost unnoticeable gift for each of us.
    Oftentimes overlooked by fear,
    apathy,
      or whatever seems to precede living.
I am a sponge who wears prescription sunglasses,
    shading eyes that just have to stare.
    Being easily entertained,
      educated
        and quickly intrigued,
        by what we think
        and how we behave as human beings.
My mother never realized she raised a
    Tse va ho,
    someone not afraid to stare.
From the pastels iridescent
    in reds
      purples
        and oranges,
        washing daily the skies above Waeh Sa Poo.
To the arch women easily curve into
    as they bend
    to gather cooking wood,
    or a crying baby.
Finding irony in women who
    perch precariously on high heels,
      during icy,
      winter months.

    Absorbing the tragic desecration of our land,
      as beer cans are thoughtlessly tossed
      from passing cars.

An Intellectual
from Tuba City

Witnessing children's confusion,
        their questions hushed by
        preoccupied adults,
        as youthful wonder clouds
        into inhibition.
        Yet, I see the same children,
        moving grandparents to tears of joy,
        by simply laughing.
All of this gets soaked up,
        storing in a chamber
        called my heart
        and when the sponge is full,
            it gets wrung out.
        Wrung out into these clay forms you see.
        wrung out into these words I offer you.

PEARLENE AND FRIENDS

PEARLENE

Pearlene has never been the kind of person
  who hides the truth of her character,
  a real woman,
     right down to her purple tennies.
Back home the women gossip openly about Pearlene,
  "What kind of Pueblo girl is she?
  Wearing tight-fitted skirts
  high above her knees."
  The women smirk,
  each waiting to speak their mind.
  "Why, she doesn't even know how to use her punte,
  poor thing,
  what kind of man would marry a girl
  who can't even bake bread?"
  Finally, the women disband after their fill of gossip.
Although when night falls,
  and darkness welcomes fantasy,
  there are Pueblo men daring enough
  to knock on Pearlene's door.
  Asking in sinful whispers,
  "Can we go to the canyon in my new truck?"
  Such naughty invitations from men,
  whose wives love Pearlene
  as their main staple in gossip.
Don't let that carefree walk fool you,
  Pearlene is a no-nonsense,
  hardworking Pueblo woman
  who tells each suitor
  single or married,
  she will accept a ride
  only on her own terms.

When the trucks return,
    safely parked in their yards, again,
    Pearlene will patiently wait
    for just the right knock.

Pearlene's Date

62

Pearlene Teaching
Her Cousins Poker

Pearlene has two aunts,
    Celestine and Virgie.
    Brown,
      round
    Tewa matriarchs
      who see their niece
      as a pitiful example
      of a Pueblo woman.
It's a good thing
    loyalty is a virtue
    among matriarchs,
    otherwise,
    Pearlene would
      have her share of problems.
Both aunts pray
    for their niece,
    believing,
      eventually
      she will return to tradition,
      leaving behind
        youthful nonsense.
    In the meantime,
      both aunts
      enjoy
      the universal pastime,
        gossip.
Preparing the adobe oven
    for bread baking,
    Aunt Celestine,
      always first to speak
    demands,

63

"Pearlene should be ashamed,
running wild into the night
toward a place called 'Vegas.'
Spending days there,
throwing good money away
on card games."
There is silence,
as Aunt Virgie
stirs the fire,
blazing in the oven.
Persisting,
Aunt Celestine continues,
"Our other sisters
began lighting candles
for their niece,
when hearing
she took
to dancing
until dawn
blinded her
card-crazed eyes."
By now Celestine
was hot,
not only from the oven,
cleaned and mopped,
ready for baking.
Aunt Virgie
handed her sister
dough,
shaped in large buns.
Celestine,
stuffing loaves

quickly on the floor
  of the oven,
    continued.
"It's all our faults,
we let Pearlene
go wild,
now look at her,
teasing the men,
bringing card games
into the village.
Playing poker."
Virgie
busy,
sealing the oven door
with flagstone
draped in wet cloth.
As if her sister
had never baked before,
Celestine
stressed the importance
of steam
in properly
cooking
  moist,
    high-rising bread.
In the same breath,
she continued to criticize Pearlene . . .
"Se kana sena wi din ha ginna pi,
wi kwee da na muu . . .
poor men, they don't know
she's a flirt."

Virgie
  pulled the last
  loaves from
  the mud oven,
  vapor rose,
  sending
  the sweet aroma
  of fresh bread
  toward the village.
Spent from gossip,
  Celestine
  let Virgie
  butter the top of each loaf
  and wrap them safely
  in pink-flowered cloth.
Signaling
  by a glance,
  their jobs done,
  both matriarchs
  returned home.
Thoughtfully,
  Aunt Virgie
  sliced warm bread
  for dinner,
    secretly wishing
    to be Pearlene
    for just one night.

"Damn it," Pearlene swore out loud.
    "I hate nylons that sag."
    Winking into the mirror,
    examining
    and adjusting makeup
    on that once
    perfect,
       youthful face.
    A face betraying her,
    telling signs of age,
    too many men
      and long nights
         at nameless bars.
Listening to Pearlene's stories,
    believing,
    at forty
      she'd seen her share of life.
    Hands on those generous hips,
    allowing the luxury
    of memory,
reliving
    youthful days,
    wishfully whispering,
    "You should of seen me."
It was hard to imagine
    Pearlene's roots,
    where she'd come from,
    with her
    passion-blue eye shadow
    and graying bouffant.
    A Pueblo woman
    boasting an arm tattoo

67

reading "Jimmy forever,"
black and bold
on dark skin,
a lark Pearlene
    chanced
        in one of those nameless bars.
She was a Towa,
    beneath that veneer
    of Avon
        and fast,
            hard times.
Signs of her Pueblo roots
surface,
    crooning
        in thoughtful
            respectful songs.
While picking herbs
    from along the highway
    plants that would heal herself
        and others.
Even the way Pearlene walks,
    in those black,
        open-toed heels
            with a gracefulness
                that could only be gifted
                    by the cloud people.
Pearlene belongs
    to a timeless tradition
        connecting her
            and other Towa
                to their roots.

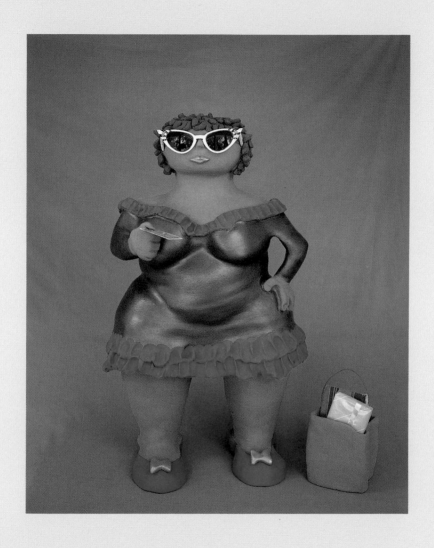

Pearlene's Roots

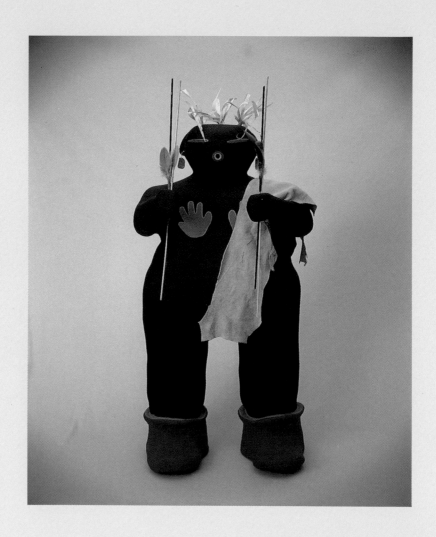

70

Moonlight

MOONLIGHT

The men called him Moonlight.
    Everyone knows him
    especially the women,
    old,
    young
    and lonely,
    are helpless to his charm.
Appearing only at night,
    around firelit dances,
    or in the canyons,
    where romance
    goes undisturbed.
It isn't bad
    if you pass,
    eyes averted,
    but if Moonlight
    catches the glint
    in your eye,
        you have no choice,
        but to surrender.
Starting with shameless stares
    past imperfections
    and loneliness,
    inviting you into
    hushed conversations
    of fantasies
        he knows
            you know exist.
As word spreads
    about Moonlight,
    women fear
    they too will

be seduced.
Leaving,
after morning
reminds women
of the night before,
when his fingers
moved slightly
against their breast,
tracing the curves
of a neck.
Passionately whispering
into uncoiled hair,
calling women closer
to his shadows
where sounds
explode deep
inside their anxious bodies.
No wonder the woman feared him,
    never being the same
    after one night
    under the Moonlight.
    Fantasies revealed
        husbands useless
            lonely bodies
                eagerly waiting
                    for another night of passion.
In their fearful anger,
    men speak
    of stopping Moonlight.
    Impossible.
    He simply takes refuge
    during the day.

Moonlight slips smoothly
    into the working woman's routine,
    becoming a lingering gaze
    from a young mother's
    kitchen window.
      A fleeting smile
        crossing an otherwise
          serious
            accepting face.
The men call him Moonlight,
    everyone knows him. . . .

Coyote smiled,
    boasting flirtatious intentions,
    under the silhouette
      of a crescent moon.
    Impatiently pacing,
      near the creek,
        sprung from Blue Lake waters.
Coyote waits,
    under wooden wrungs,
    as women whisper
    descending a ladder in graceful forms.
    Draped,
      their shawls' fringe swaying,
        brushing against
          the wet of his nose.
Coyote can't help himself,
    blurting romantic suggestions
      to each woman as she descends the ladder.
Tonight he goes unnoticed.
    There are other things these women must do,
      grinding the fall harvest
        waiting the men's return
          keeping the fires burning.
Inattention sets his swagger straight,
    the cocky smile gone.
Coyote intentions,
    just a dream,
      and now you know why he howls alone.

75

Happy To Just
Be a Thing

A WELL-TRAVELED COYOTE

John F. Kennedy
New York City
I saw him across the lobby
flight 161
St. Louis
Albuquerque.
Coyote looked in control
cool
fitting right into the city
smiling when a pretty woman passed him
figuring out his flight
making calculations from behind
the *New York Times.*
Slick
right down to his Tony Lamas
Coyote
I'd recognize him anywhere
Copenhagen
New York
Gallup.
People say
you can dress 'em up
but once a coyote
always a coyote.

*A Well-Traveled
Coyote*

HOME

Thung joo Kwa yaa na povi sah
Thung joo Kwa yaa na povi sah
   Tsay ohi taa geh wo gi wa naa povi sah
   pin povi
   pin povi do mu u da kun
   ka nee na nun dun naa da si tah.
On top of Black Mesa there are flowers
On top of Black Mesa there are flowers
   dew on yellow flowers
   mountain flowers I see
   so far away that it makes me cry.
She opened her eyes slowly,
   as if to awaken from a trance
      cast by a song,
      transporting her to childhood,
   Back to the flowers
   growing atop Black Mesa,
   so far and yet
   clearly brilliant.
Awake from the song,
   Gia focused on her daughter,
   anxiously awaiting
   to be taught a new song.
The old woman chose to take her time,
   she had learned from experience,
   attention is better paid by children,
   when there is a little pause,
      and mystery
         in storytelling.
Soon enough Gia spoke . . .
   "When I was a young girl,

my family would camp
below Kwheng sa po,
during the farming months.
We spent most of our days
following my grandmother
through rows of corn
and playing in the streams below.
One day white men came in a wagon,
telling us about a school for Indians,
run by the government.
We were told this school would educate
and prepare us for jobs in the white man's world.
None of us knew what any of it meant,
but these men spoke sweetly
offering grandmother a roll of baling wire
for each child that went to school.
Before we knew what was happening,
we were sitting in the back of their wagon,
on our way to government school,
away from our families,
to another man's world.
Often we would cry,
out of loneliness,
but this song helped us
to remember our home."
Gia thoughtfully straightened
the pleats on her skirt,
swallowing the last of her coffee.
Smiling, she continued . . .

"The government school taught sewing,
I learned on an electric machine.

83

Gia and Daughter

By the time I returned to the village I could
sew, but few of the people had heard of sewing machines,
or even electricity.
The machine I learned to operate as my trade
could not be carried here and there,
but this song you are learning,
will always be carried in your heart,
here and there."

SOMETIMES SHE JUST SITS

Sometimes she'll sit,
    under the willow,
    on days of celebration
    in the village.
A matriarch,
    a mother of many
    and a wife
      going on fifty years.
Her days of duty
    demanding
      constant motion
        are over.
Earning her place
    under the willow,
    as younger matriarchs
    prepare food,
    baking bread,
    stirring stews
      and welcoming
      hungry guests.
Men,
    women
    and children
    corn dancers,
    dressed in
    ceremonial cloth
    of red
      black
        and green,
          grasping evergreen
            and freshly harvested,
              colored corn.

86

Sometimes
She Just Sits

Passing the matriarch,
dancers
nod respectfully
while moving
toward the
Pueblo's center.
Satisfied
     with her prominence,
          she smiles
Remembering
     her once
     youthful grace
     on the days
     she lifted
     her feet
          to dance.
     Blessed corn
     and evergreen
          raised toward
               the blue womb
                    above her.
Drum sounds,
     inviting
     her beyond
          the day
               its crowd
                    and heat,
                         to the center
                              of her people,
                                   where the spirit world begins.   **87**

She sits
    in the airport
    watching people
    check their luggage,
    missing flights,
    meeting friends.
A forty-year-old
    mother of two,
    divorced,
    lonely,
    sitting
    in the haven
    of a dimly lit lounge.
    She's noticeable
    in the crowd
    of hard-drinking
    businessmen
    and loud marines.
Quietly perched
on a bar stool,
shapely legs crossed,
her body,
    lean
    and still youthful.
Waiting a flight call
filling empty time
for mind travel,
past her morning martini
and cigarette

    smoldering
    between her polished nails.

Thinking of past husbands,
a present lover,
growing children.
A thoughtful moment
of pleasure
    melts an empty stare,
    smiling
    she checks her watch.
A stranger flirts
moments before her flight,
    she waves him away.
Gathering herself,
cigarettes and coat
she steadies her walk
    toward the gate
      of the plane,
        waiting to whisk
        her into
          the open
            cloudless skies.

90

A Sister's Dream

A SISTER'S DREAM

Flying
    the seven of us
        taking turns gliding
            along
                against pale blue
                    cloudless skies.
Sisters
    making sewing motions
        around
        above
            under.
So smooth
    and easy
        in weightlessness
            above mother's watchful eye
                growing for us
                    Pinon
                        Sage
                          Chokecherries.
The seven of us
    flying
        along asphalt highways
            laughing contagiously
                celebrating our friendship
                and love
                    toward our mother
                      awaiting our arrival
                    with open
                      expansive
                        sheltering wings.

We coiled each row with mud bricks,
    lifting,
        measuring,
            shaping one adobe at a time.
This earth vessel
    rounded into rooms
        we raise our children in.
Staggered bricks of straw
    mud and sand
    like the Towa before us
    who sculpted
    their own shelters
    upward
    in basic
        uneven layers
            one adobe at a time.
In our vessel
    there are thousands of adobes
    anchored to a solid bed of concrete,
    evenly distributing the weight
        of walls seventeen feet high.
Greg designed
    our cradle of packed earth,
    keeping with the adobe tradition
    of simple,
        wavering lines,
        that move quietly,
        curving in and out of rooms
            one after another.
92   Plastering,
    molding
        and repacking

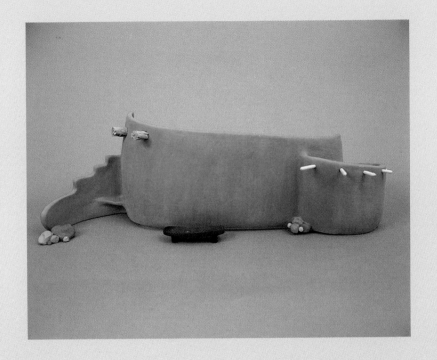

Home

an endless supply of bricks,
until our mud shell
stood upright
massive
and invincible.
Sounds easily surrender
to walls absorbing
the details of our lives.
Coughs from sick children
romantic whispers
and heated debates,
all digested into
porous layers of mortar.
I shake my head thinking,
"Only earth mother
would permit such a burden,
allowing us to dig foundations
into her skin
and forgiving us the weight
of tons and tons of mass,
yet, holding us safe and steady."
Our vessel made from
her brown
solid skin.
Earth mother,
giving all that she is,
one adobe at a time.

What Happens
to Indian Kids
When They Watch
Too Much TV

CHILDREN

I cannot remember
    when I was without my children's love.
    When there weren't cries at midnight
        for a bottle,
        or a diaper change,
        disrupting precious sleep.
    Waking to children's persistence
        for cereal
        before dawn
        on a Saturday morning.
    Strategically planning an escape
        to the bathroom
        for five minutes
        of uninterrupted peace,
    Appreciating the gift of silence
        while sleeping twins recharge.
Yet, these children
    awaken my curious nature,
    humorously dissolving
        my stubborn anger.
    Their direct intuition
        and truthful manner
        astounds me.
I am enlightened
    by these wonders,
    whose mere presence
    can be nothing less than magic
        pure and simple magic.

MY FATHER'S HANDS

I have hands like my father,
    always in motion.
    Stirring sugared coffee
    before hoeing his rows of beans.
    He grew the best chili,
        the hottest were his pride,
        pointing to the fresh ones,
        he'd laugh and say,
        "Hot and mean like me."
He was stabbed once in a fight
    in the center of his right palm,
    damaging his fingers,
    that never fully healed.
    His middle finger slanted stiffly inward,
    though his grip remained firm.
Such steady hands my father had,
    carving
    past midnight
    into Gia's black bowls
    Drawing perfect lines
    in delicate strokes,
    a simple pocketknife his only tool.
His were the hands that lifted me,
    when I was just a girl,
    tugging playfully at my hair,
    that curled behind my ear.
    His hands,
    narrow and skilled,
    copper colored and calloused,
    weather chapped and strong.

I have hands like my father,
    I know this myself,
        but like hearing my daughter say so.

99

Man and Bird
Singing

It would begin in the early morning,
    on any given day.
    His feet would hit the floor
      with such definite purpose,
      even though his day's routine
      had not yet been calculated.
    His thump echoing,
      crossing closets,
      space and bodies.
    We rose
        as if that sound signaled
        our day's start.
    The bugles of morning,
      my father's feet.
Rise children
    and have purpose.

    Making our thumps heard,
      smaller feet hitting cold pine,
      the impact forcing our day upon us.
    It was this way,
      every day.
There were three pairs of boots
    standing at attention,
    in the corner of his room.
    On Sunday morning,
    he would slip
    into his spit-polished,
      hand-tooled,
        Mexican leather boots.
          These were his favorite,

101

Yuppie Yazzies

Although he prized
his practical hunting lace-ups,
methodically woven together
by cowhide cut in strips.
These were not to be mistaken
for the ordinary,
   lesser polished
     work-day
       dog kickers.
His children were well familiar
with each set of boots,
   their importance
     and occasion
       each pair was worn.
Time has passed,
   my father's feet gnarled
    by an untimely stroke.
   His arches fallen
making the usual shifting of weight
   from one foot
     to the next,
       painful
        and awkward.
Shu nave ung din hee.
Oh my feet hurt.
   He says this
   as I kneel,
   cupping one foot
    at a time.
   Kneading lifeless muscles
    as if to beg them
     back to life.

I listen to the distance
   he travels
     now,
       only by memory.
Coating his feet with lotion,
hoping to retard
   the atrophy
     developed by illness
       and inactivity.
Ha wa
ha wa
   Momentarily comforted,
   his words determine
     my hand pressure,
       for I wish only to heal him.
   I sit by his bed,
   noticing
     from across the room,
     the boots he once wore,
     still at attention,
       unnoticed,
         unworn,
           left to collect dust.
It's then I remember . . .
   the early call of morning,
     on any given day.
His feet would hit the floor
   with such a definite purpose.

104

Ta

I asked about success
    how was I to measure it,
    struggling in
    two worlds,
        between Pueblo tradition
        and modern values.
    Keeping on course,
        a balance
        of who I am
            and wish to become.
Ta took his time answering.
    I thought maybe
        he hadn't heard,
        or worse,
        not listened.
    Waiting
        I noticed,
        how time
        had tailored my father
        into an old man
        wrinkled
            and halting.
    Finally,
        with clear
        thoughtful words,
        my father spoke:
        "Navi a yu,
        hi wu na mang,
        uvi aa yaa,
        uvi seng,
        da hihchan po o.
        Navi a yu,

hi wodi kwee un muu,
oe to jan be,
hi wo na mang,
sa wo na mang."
"My daughter,
it is going well,
your children,
your husband,
are happy.
My daughter,
you are a good woman,
listen,
it is going well,
it goes in beauty."
Simple
   words,
      reminding me,
      success
      is not only
      respecting tradition
      or balancing
      modern values.
      It is the appreciation
      of life's basic gifts,
      weaving
      into the whole
      of who you are
      and who you can become.
Ta sat under the Elm,
   drifting to sleep
      his hand in mine.

OE KHEE UNG

Ta da oe khee ung
    Kung ye ung meng.
Father get ready,
    you have far to travel.
Keep your gaze steady
    beyond starched
      white sheets
    Tucked neatly by
      attentive nurses.
    Past these ordinary,
      colorless,
        sterile walls,
          that can no longer contain you.
    Unhooking your IV
      when night signals,
      releasing yourself
      to stand straight
      and strong,
        again.
Oe khee ung
    Kung ye ung meng
Ta Povi waits by the canyon's rim
inviting you to walk with him
past the fields
    you both planted
      seasons ago.
Toward Kwheng sa po,
near the clearing,
    where Sparrow's nest
    and Autumn leaves
    gather to bed doe
      and fawn.

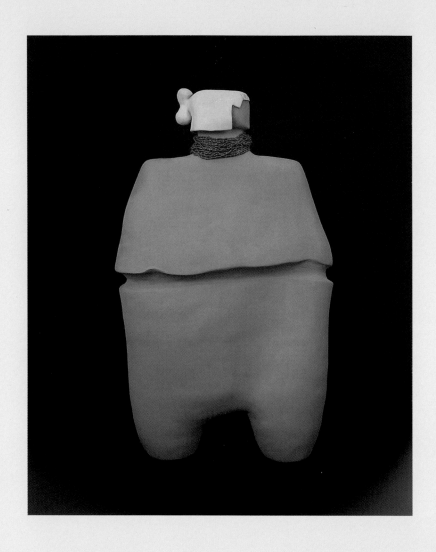

108

Oe khee ung
or All Men

Ta Povi calls from the Aspen
    near the meadow
    by your mother's breast.
With ceremony,
    rain clouds welcoming you,
      healing shadows
        erasing your pain.
Oe khee ung
    get ready to cross
    into the canyon's rim.
Making a place for yourself
    near the sagebrush
    along the wolf trails
    where you have always
      been at home.
In time,
    it will be you calling me,
    inviting me toward the canyon's rim,
    near the road we carved
      above the timberline
        many winters ago.

110

Morning Ritual

CLAY RITUALS

Each morning I stretch
 upward,
  greeting the sun,
   climbing into
    Eastern skies.
Steaming coffee
cooling quickly
 in cold mugs.
Children,
refreshed,
 exchanging dreams
  from their beds.
These seemingly ordinary rituals
 add to my day,
 figuring prominently
 into the larger scheme
  of things,
   for me.
I am comfortable
 with daily ceremonies.
 Opening the studio door,
 calling on memory
 to remind my hands,
 where I left off
  from yesterday's work.
Senge Taa muu,
 words of greeting
 a new day
 reflects off
 clay forms
 in various stages
  of readiness.

There are sounds
    dancing within these walls,
    telling of
    air bubbles bursting
    while surfacing
    in mud soup.
    The noise of clay,
    being slapped
    back and forth,
    rythmically,
      from one hand
        to the next.
    Even stubborn cracks
    have sounds
    when opening
      into irreparable canyons.
Daily ceremonies
    that quietly extol,
    all things as they are,
      each being as valuable
        as the next.
    Morning stretches,
    clay sounds
    and my children's dreams,
    daily rituals
      reminding me to celebrate.

PIT FIRING A MILESTONE

The promises of a clear,
    calm day
    fooled me into thinking
    the time was right.
    Right
      for the firing of my bowl
        and what was to be
          a milestone in my life.
Only one form
    was to be fired,
      by hot
        quick
          Cedar flames,
            in the crisp,
              still air.
This bowl,
    my redemption,
    would prove
    once and for all,
    especially to me,
    that symmetrical vessels
    standard in Pueblo tradition
    lived on
      in this modern
        Tewa woman.
    Although
    I could not explain
    the method in which
    I accomplished this feat,
I feared my bowl
    a fluke,

this thought fueled my determination
    to fire.
Gia once told me
    firing was best
    before dawn.
    The night's memory
    still fresh
    the air languid
      and peaceful,
      before the wind
        kicks up his heels.
Waiting for weeks
    looking for a sign,
    permission,
    that would promise
      a smokeless,
        clean firing.
It would be today,
    although as yet,
    I could not bring myself
    to say the word,
    fire,
    fearing the mere utterance was taboo.
For older
    wiser potters,
    this firing
    would have been done
    weeks ago,
    but I am young
    and have not mastered
      clay's secrets.

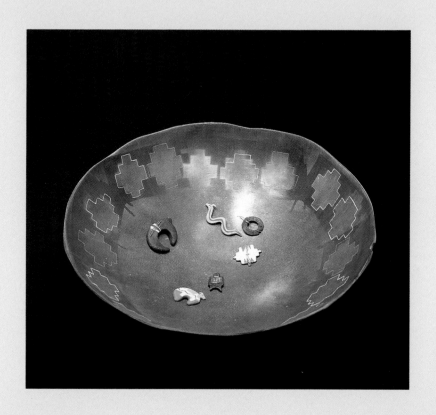

115

Old, New
Medicine Bowl

Digging a four-foot hole
    in the ground,
    I made plans to fire.
    Thinking,
    how ironic
    this last step
    of many stages,
    determined
        months of work.
My neighbor openly stared,
    leisurely drinking coffee,
    hot pink rollers
    dotting her hair
    as she watched
        her curious neighbor
            dig a mysterious pit.
The logistics of firing
    a large mass of clay
    in this crude oven
    worried me.
    Heat
    rising quickly
    from split
        dry Cedar,
        would need to burn evenly.
    A calm day
would be essential
    for fire smoke
    to escape
116   upward,
        away from the bowl itself.

Covering the entire floor
     with split Juniper,
     I layered the earth oven
     with a succession of
     wood,
     a thick metal grate
     used to shoulder
     the weight of clay,
     more wood
     and finally,
     a sheet of protective tin.
     All this,
     for a single bowl
     with an opening
     the length of my arm.
     Paper thin walls
     that fanned out
     from a circular base,
     no larger than my hand.
The audience grew,
     even our dogs
     sensed the importance
     of this occasion.
     Keeping a safe distance
     yet,
       never looking away from the pit.
While carefully
     setting the bowl
     on a sturdy metal grate,
     the slightest
     suggestion of wind
     breezed through my hair.

I froze momentarily,
considering the situation.
I'd spent months
shaping,
tenderly packing
and nurturing
my bowl,
yet,
I was willing
to sacrifice her
in a moment of impatience,
to the Gods of weather.
I thought of Gia,
wondering what she
would have done.
I am young
and impatient.
I lit the Cedar.
Watching the flames
erupt,
sparks jetted upward
landing as glowing embers
near my feet,
my heartbeat
near the front of my collar.
Several minutes passed,
sporadic drops
soon turned into
a steady sheet
118   of rain.
Soaked
and helpless,

I witnessed
the explosion of fire
whimper,
    to struggling coals.
It poured,
    for two days,
    turning the top layer
    of pit
    into a paste
    of ash and mud.
    For days
    I mourned,
    feeling betrayed,
    eyeing the pit,
    yet unable to
    examine the damage.
    Several dogs sniffed cautiously,
    around the muddy hole.
    My children asked
    about the bowl,
    in hushed tones,
    as if speaking of a relative
      that has passed on.
    It was then,
    I decided to face
    the truth.
Shovel in hand
I began digging mud
from the surface,
feeling the heat
escaping
toward my face.

I realized,
the pit was warm
from an inner source
of heat.
Hands gloved
in protective leather,
cleared away
remaining layers.
Fingers numb
from anticipation
wiped tears
clouding my view,
the layer of protection
enveloped and shielded
flames within the pit,
firing the bowl
slowly
        for days.
Completely unearthed
        and whole
        Micaceous flecks
        glistened against
        dark shadows,
        cast by Cedar smoke
        unable to escape upward,
        delicately dotting
        the fired surface
        with beautiful
        cloudlike formations.
Everything changed,
        the air seemed lighter

the burden of worry
lifted.
The dogs resumed
playful activity.
The children sighed,
welcoming our
relative back to life.
My neighbor faded
behind closing curtains,
possibly protecting herself
from this curious woman
across the field
on all fours
   caked in mud
      witnessing the birth
         of her milestone.

Sculpture Specifications

Heeng chae Kosa, p. 3
25″h × 11″w
Micaceous clay, 1990
From the collection of Michael Gann
Photo by Mary Fredenburgh

Mud Fetish, p. 21
10″h × 2″w
Santa Clara clay, 1975
From the collection of the
   Wheelwright Museum
Photo by Addison Doty

**Pinto Bean and Grasshopper
Ate My Lilacs and Didn't Even
Care,** p. 22
Pinto Bean, *left* 21″h × 8″w
Grasshopper, *right* 26″h × 10″w
Santa Clara clay, 1980
Photo by Mary Fredenburgh

Landscape, p. 25
11″h × 10½″w
Santa Clara clay, 1982
Photo by Mary Fredenburgh

Flat Fetishes, p. 26
Fetish *left* 12″h × 6″w
Fetish *right* 14″h × 8″w

Santa Clara clay, 1990
Photo by Mary Fredenburgh

**Kosa (Pueblo Clowns) Poking
Fun,** p. 29
Kosa with camera 6″h × 2″w
Waving Kosa 6″h × 2″w
Santa Clara clay, 1978
From the collection of Charles and
   Carol Gurke
Photo by Mary Fredenburgh

**Water Jar on Mud Woman's
Head,** p. 32
40″h × 15″w
Micaceous clay, Summer 1991
From the collection of Charles and
   Carol Gurke
Photo by Mary Fredenburgh

**Mud Woman's First Encounter
with the World of Money and
Business,** p. 34
38″h × 16″w
Micaceous clay, 1987
From the Heard Museum collection
Photo by Mary Fredenburgh

From the collection of Jeff and
   Laurie Zimmerman
Photo by Mary Fredenburgh

Gia and Daughter, p. 83
Gia 36″h × 18″w
Micaceous clay, 1989
From the collection of Carl Stern
   and Holly Hayes
Daughter 25″h × 16″w
Micaceous clay, 1989
From the collection of Arlene
   Anastos
Photo by Mary Fredenburgh

Sometimes She Just Sits, p. 86
16″h × 10½″w
Bronze, No. 5 in an edition of 10
Photo by Mary Fredenburgh

A Sister's Dream, p. 90
36″h × 18″w
Micaceous clay, 1988
From the collection of Ken Bailey
Photo by Mary Fredenburgh

Home, p. 93
12½″l × 5″h
Micaceous clay, 1991
From the artist's collection
Photo by Mary Fredenburgh

**What Happens to Indian Kids
When They Watch Too Much
TV,** p. 95
Couch 12″l × 6″w
Children 3″l × 1½″w

TV 3″h × 3″w
Micaceous and Santa Clara clays,
   1986
From the Collection of Jim Evers
Photo by Mary Fredenburgh

Man and Bird Singing, p. 99
30″h × 12″w
Santa Clara clay, 1988
From the collection of Nancy
   Morris
Photo by Mary Fredenburgh

Yuppie Yazzies, p. 101
Father 36″h × 16″w
Son 18″h × 12″w
Dog 16″l × 7″h
Micaceous clay, 1989
From the collection of Mr. and Mrs.
   David Lieberman
Photo by Mary Fredenburgh

Ta, p. 104
Ta 2½″h × 1″w
House 9″h × 9½″w
Santa Clara clay, 1985
From the collection of Charles and
   Carol Gurke
Photo by Addison Doty

Oe khee ung or All Men, p. 108
45″h × 22″w
Micaceous and Santa Clara clays,
   1990
Photo by Mary Fredenburgh

Morning Ritual, p. 110
22″h × 8″w
Micaceous clay, 1989
From the collection of Jim Evers
Photo by Mary Fredenburgh

Old, New Medicine Bowl, p. 115
11″h × 35″w
Micaceous clay, 1988
From the collection of The Museum
   of Northern Arizona
Photo by Gene Balzer

ABOUT THE AUTHOR

Nora Naranjo-Morse says of the time that she first picked up a lump of clay: "I'll never forget that . . . I just started feeling it, and I knew that was the time." She still gathers her own clay near her home in Española, New Mexico. She considers this work part of the creative process. Of the characters she molds she says, "They are all of us. . . . Even people I don't know who say something to me or turn their heads in a certain way or have a certain look become very important in what goes into the character."

In addition to having taught the techniques of Santa Clara Pueblo pottery throughout the American West, Denmark, and Germany, Nora Naranjo-Morse has exhibited her work in galleries all around the country and has published her poetry in books such as the *Ceremony of Brotherhood* (1981), *A Gathering of Spirits* (1982), and *Sun Tracks*, and in journals such as *Fireweed*.